Violin Exam Pieces

ABRSM Grade 7

Selected from the 2012–2015 syllabus

Name

Date

CW00665465

CD

Violin & Piano Piano only

Contents

Violin consultant: Philippa Bunting

Footnotes: Edward Huws Jones (EHJ), Richard Jones (RJ) and Anthony Burton

Other pieces for Grade 7

First published in 2011 by ABRSM (Publishing) Ltd, a wholly owned subsidiary of ABRSM, 24 Portland Place, London W1B 1LU, United Kingdom
© 2011 by The Associated Board of the Royal Schools of Music

Music origination by Andrew Jones
Cover by Økvik Design
Printed in England by Halstan & Co. Ltd, Amersham, Bucks.

Adagio

First movement from Sonata in G, BWV 1021

J. S. Bach

Edited by Peter Wollny
Continuo realization by
Zvi Meniker
Fingering and bowing by
Andrew Manze

The great German composer Johann Sebastian Bach (1685–1750) composed a large quantity of sacred music, much of it for the churches in Leipzig where he spent the last 27 years of his life, and also music for keyboard and for different instrumental combinations. His surviving works for violin and harpsichord, his own two principal instruments, include six sonatas with fully written-out keyboard parts, but also two others with a 'continuo' accompaniment in the form of a bass line with figures indicating the harmonies to be filled in above it. This is the first movement of one of the continuo accompanied sonatas. The work was copied out by Bach's wife Anna Magdalena in the early 1730s, although it may have been written several years earlier. It seems to have formed part of Bach's teaching, since the figuring of the bass line is unusually detailed, and the same bass was used for two other works stemming from Bach's circle of family and pupils. This edition includes one possible 'realization' of the keyboard part by Zvi Meniker. It also includes fingering and bowing by Andrew Manze, which is based on what we know of the practice of Bach's time, but which he says represents 'information rather than instruction', for a player to adapt as necessary. The appoggiaturas in bars 7, 13 and 15 should be played on the beat, as part of the melody. Dynamics are left to the player's discretion.

A Soldier's Resolution

A:2

Arranged by Edward Huws Jones

Tobias Hume

Tobias Hume (*c.*1579–1645) was an English composer and viol player, and a professional soldier. 'A Soldier's Resolution' comes from his collection *Captain Hume's Musical Humours*, which was published in 1605. Pieces such as this, forming musical descriptions of battles, were popular throughout the 16th century and into the 17th century, and included Monteverdi's *Combattimento di Tancredi e Clorinda* and Susato's *Battle Pavane*. Hume's collection uses various devices and effects, including *col legno* ('Drum this with the backe of the Bow') and *pizzicato* ('Play…with your finger'), and it is appropriate to use these in this piece. Hume does not directly indicate harmonics but the technique, with its trumpet-like sound, was familiar at the time and is used to good effect in bars 84–94. For the three- and four-note chords, experiment with different ways of playing, including single-note spreads. The piece calls for strongly-characterized playing, with vivid contrasts of tempo, dynamics and articulation. In this arrangement the piece has been transposed up a 4th from D to G, the fuller bass viol chords have been adapted for the violin and an unobtrusive keyboard accompaniment has been added. EHJ

6

The Second Part
The Kettle Drum

90

p

93

f

mf

Pell-mell

♩ = c.66   **accel.**

96

mf pesante

As fast as possible ♩ = c.120

103

f   *cresc.*

ff

March Away

Tempo I

110

mf detached

118   pizz.

p   *dim. al fine*

A:3

Allegro

First movement from Concerto in A minor, Op. 3 No. 6, RV 356

Edited by and continuo realized by
Richard Jones

Antonio Vivaldi

The Venetian composer Antonio Vivaldi (1678–1741) was ordained as a priest in 1703 – he was known as 'the red priest' on account of his red hair. Later in the same year he was appointed *maestro di violino* at the Pio Ospedale della Pietà in Venice, a girls' orphanage that specialized in musical training. Vivaldi's first collection of concertos, *L'estro armonico*, Op. 3, from which this Allegro is taken, was first published in Amsterdam in 1711. The collection was highly influential throughout Europe and brought great fame to its composer. RJ

In the exam the violinist should play the tutti sections as well as the solo sections.

Source: *L'estro armonico*, Op. 3 (Amsterdam: Roger, 1711)

B:1

Spanischer Tanz

No. 2 from *Spanische Tänze*, Op. 12

Arranged by Philipp Scharwenka

Moritz Moszkowski

Moritz Moszkowski (1854–1925) was born in the German city of Breslau (now Wrocław in Poland) and was educated in Dresden and Berlin. As a young man he enjoyed a successful career as a concert pianist, but illness later forced him to concentrate on conducting and teaching. He was also a prolific composer, chiefly for the piano: he wrote both virtuoso pieces for the recital platform and music for the domestic market. His five *Spanish Dances*, Op. 12, for piano duet, published in 1876, were immensely popular with amateur pianists in the 19th and early 20th centuries. The second of the set is in moderate waltz time, with some Spanish melodic and harmonic inflections. This arrangement is by the Polish-German composer Philipp Scharwenka (1847–1917), elder brother of the pianist-composer Xaver Scharwenka, and a teaching colleague of Moszkowski in Berlin.

Source: *Spanische Tänze*, Op. 12 (C. F. Peters, n. d.)

Allegro vivace

Third movement from Sonatina in D, Op. 137 No. 1, D. 384

Edited by Günter Henle and Karl Röhrig
Fingering and bowing by
Karl Röhrig

Franz Schubert

Franz Schubert (1797–1828) was born in the suburbs of Vienna, the capital of the Austro-Hungarian Empire, and lived in the city for virtually all of his short life. He is famous chiefly for his hundreds of songs, but he also composed operas, choral music, orchestral works, music for piano and chamber music. For violin and piano – two instruments which he learned as a child – he wrote four sonatas, a Rondo and a Fantasy. The first three sonatas all date from March and April 1816, shortly after his 19th birthday. Schubert may have hoped to get them published as a set, but if so he was disappointed: they appeared in print only after his death, in 1836. They were published under the title 'Sonatinas', 'little sonatas', presumably because of their relatively compact dimensions but perhaps also to increase their appeal to students and amateurs: the title has stuck, but it is not Schubert's. This springy rondo is the finale of the first of the three. Its melodic material is shared roughly equally between the players, so the violinist must be aware of when he or she is accompanying the piano. The recurring ornament in the main tune – an acciaccatura or 'short appoggiatura' – should be played *on* rather than before the beat.

AB 3586

Mélodie

No. 3 from *Souvenir d'un lieu cher*, Op. 42

Edited by Richard Jones

P. I. Tchaikovsky

The great Russian composer Pyotr Il'yich Tchaikovsky (1840–93) studied law in St Petersburg as a teenager, but in 1862 he entered the newly founded conservatory in that city as a pupil of Anton Rubinstein. From 1866 he taught music theory at the conservatory in Moscow. In 1876 a wealthy widow, Nadezhda von Meck, sent him a commission that resulted in her becoming his long-term patron and pen-friend. This made him financially secure and able to resign his post at the conservatory.

The three pieces of *Souvenir d'un lieu cher*, Op. 42, were composed in the spring of 1878 and are thus roughly contemporary with the Violin Concerto. The title, 'Recollection of a dear place', refers to Brailov (near Kiev), Madame von Meck's country estate, where the second and third pieces were composed. RJ

In bar 14, the fifth violin note is printed as an A♭, but is often played as an A♮. Candidates may play either note in the exam.

Source: *Souvenir d'un lieu cher*, Op. 42 (Moscow: Jurgenson, 1879)

Bagpipers
First movement from Sonatina

Transcribed by André Gertler

Béla Bartók

Béla Bartók (1881–1945) was not only one of the great composers of the 20th century, but also a pioneering collector of the folk music of his native Hungary and its neighbouring countries. His musical language was profoundly influenced by folk idioms; and many of his smaller works make use of melodies collected on his extended trips to remote country areas. For example, his Sonatina for piano of 1915 is based on Romanian melodies from the border region of Transylvania. The first movement, 'Bagpipers', uses two tunes: a round-dance which Bartók had transcribed in Hunyad county in 1913, and a melody which he had noted down in Bihar in 1910. Both were played by pipers, and Bartók's arrangement of the first tune reproduces the characteristic drone of the bagpipes in the bass of the piano. In the transcription of the Sonatina for violin and piano made in 1931 by the Hungarian-born violinist André Gertler (1907–98), a friend and regular recital partner of the composer, the drone is also represented on the violin's open D and A strings.

© 1919 by Rózsavölgyi & Co. Budapest
© Copyright assigned 1950 to Editio Musica Budapest
All enquiries about this piece, apart from those directly relating to the exams, should be addressed to Editio Musica Budapest, H-1132 Budapest, Victor Hugo u. 11–15, Hungary.

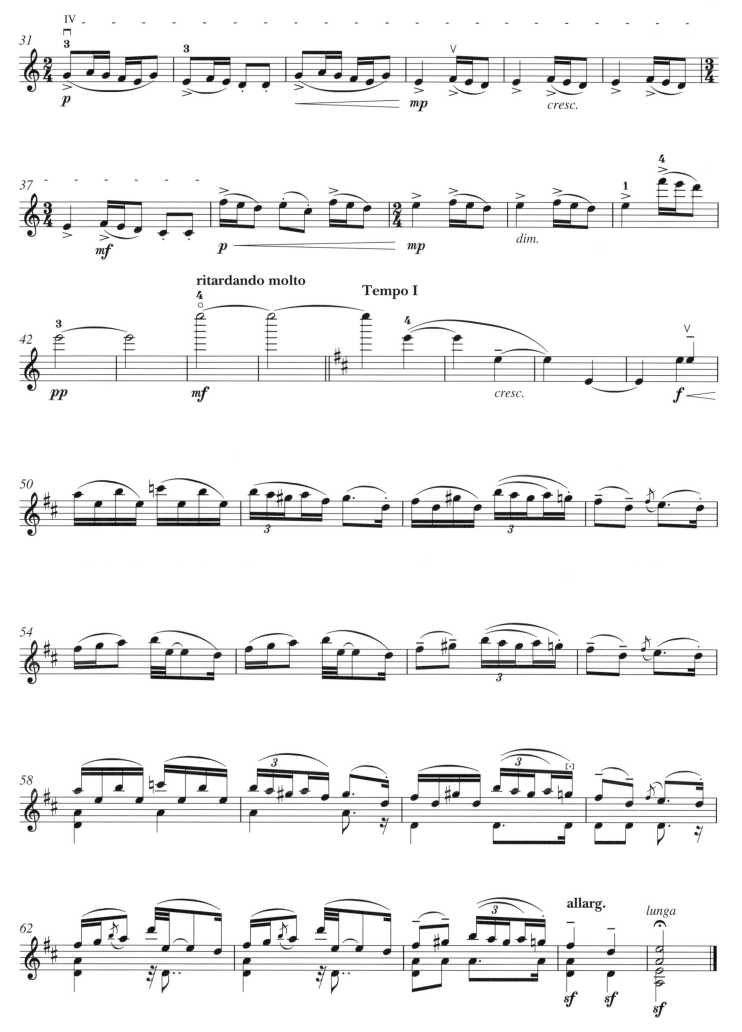

Mummenschanz

from *Much Ado About Nothing*, Op. 11

E. W. Korngold

Erich Wolfgang Korngold (1897–1957) was a child prodigy as a composer in Vienna, and had his operas produced all over Europe, before moving to Hollywood in 1934 and winning equal success writing film scores. His incidental music for Shakespeare's comedy *Much Ado About Nothing* was written for a production in the Schönbrunn Palace in Vienna in 1919: it was originally scored for chamber orchestra, but when the run of the play was extended and the orchestra was unavailable, Korngold arranged it for violin and piano, and played the piano part himself. Later he published the music both as an orchestral suite and as a suite of Four Pieces for violin and piano. The last movement of both is a *Mummenschanz*, or 'Masquerade', in the English dance rhythm of the hornpipe. The German tempo marking *bewegt* means 'with movement', *lustig* means 'merry', and *vorwärts!* is an instruction to 'get a move on'.

Published in: Vier Stücke. Aus der Musik zu Shakespeares "Viel Lärmen um nichts", ED 1927. All enquiries about this piece, apart from those directly relating to the exams, should be addressed to Schott Music Ltd, 48 Great Marlborough Street, London W1F 7BB.

C:3

for Geoffrey Allan

Reverie

Angela Morley

Angela Morley (1924–2009) was born Wally Stott in Leeds, in northern England, and under that name had a successful career as a composer, arranger and conductor, acting as musical director for the cult radio comedy series *The Goon Show* and recording with many leading singers. She continued her career in the UK and later in the USA, writing and arranging extensively for feature films (she composed most of the score of the 1978 *Watership Down*), television and concerts. Angela Morley wrote *Reverie* as a piece for violin and string orchestra in early 2005, for a broadcast on BBC Radio 3. The published score, with piano accompaniment, is dedicated to the violinist Geoffrey Allan. On her website (www.angelamorley.com), the composer wrote that she was never happy with the title of the piece, which means 'Daydream': 'Violinists, not surprisingly, play it too dreamily. I think "Romance" would have been better but my friends make a face.'